# MICHAEL SOUTHERN SR.

# Noah's Big Boat Adventure: Saving the Animals

# Contents

# Prologue

Long ago, in a world much like our own, people lived, worked, and played under the same sky and sun. But the world was not as peaceful as it could have been. Many people had forgotten about kindness, love, and the One True God who had created everything. They argued, fought, and turned away from the goodness that was meant to fill their lives. The noise of their anger and the sadness of their hearts rose up to the heavens, and the world became a place of turmoil.

But in the midst of this chaos, there was a man named Noah. Noah was different. He was a good man, a man who listened to God and followed His ways. Noah lived with his wife, his three sons, and their wives. Together, they cared for their land and their animals, and they tried to live a life of peace and kindness.

God saw Noah's goodness, and it filled His heart with joy. But God was also saddened by the way the world had become. He saw the pain, the anger, and the darkness that had spread over the earth. God knew that something needed to be done to bring the world back to its original beauty and peace.

One day, God spoke to Noah. It was a gentle, loving voice, a voice that filled Noah's heart with warmth. "Noah," God said, "I have seen the wickedness of the world, and I am saddened. I have decided to send a great flood to cleanse the earth, to wash away the evil and start anew. But I will save you, your family, and two of every kind of animal. You will build an ark, a great boat, to keep you safe through the flood. When the waters recede, you will begin a new life, filled with hope and love."

Noah listened carefully to God's words, his heart filled with a mix of awe and responsibility. He knew that this was a great task, but he also knew that he could trust God. He would do as God asked. He would build the ark, gather the animals, and trust in God's promise.

And so, Noah's journey began. It was a journey of faith, courage, and hope. It was a journey that would lead him and his family through a great storm and into a new world. This is the story of that journey, the story of Noah's Big Boat Adventure: Saving the Animals. It is a story of God's love, a love that shines as bright as a rainbow, and a promise that will never be broken.

# Introduction

In a time long, long ago, the world was a different place. It was full of people and animals, just like today. But many people had forgotten to be kind and good. They fought and argued, and they stopped listening to each other and to the One True God. The world, once so beautiful and full of life, had become a place of sadness and noise, like a storm that wouldn't go away.

But in this world of noise, there was one man who still listened to God's voice. His name was Noah. Noah was a kind man with a long, gray beard and bright eyes that sparkled with kindness. He lived with his family, and together they took care of their animals and their land. While others shouted and argued, Noah listened for the soft, gentle voice of God.

One day, as Noah was sitting under a big, shady tree, he heard that voice. It was a voice that filled his heart with warmth and love. "Noah," the voice said, "the world has become a sad place, and it must be washed clean. I will send a great flood to cover the earth, but I want you to build a big boat, an ark, to save your family and two of every kind of animal. You will keep them safe, and then we will start the world anew."

Noah's eyes widened. A flood? An ark? Save the animals? It was a lot to take in. But Noah knew that when God spoke, it was important to listen. So he nodded and stood up. He would build this ark, no matter how big or how long it took. He would save his family and the animals. He would trust in the One True God's plan.

And so, Noah began his work. He cut down tall trees and shaped the wood, making it strong and sturdy. His sons helped him, their hands busy with hammers and saws. The sound of their work echoed through the hills, a steady rhythm that filled the air. Day after day, they worked, building the ark as the sky above seemed to watch over them.

As they worked, people came to see what Noah was doing. They laughed and pointed, thinking Noah was foolish to build a boat so far from the sea. But Noah just smiled and kept working. He knew something they didn't. He knew that God had a plan, and he trusted that plan with all his heart.

Soon, the ark stood tall, a massive boat ready to sail. It was big enough for Noah's family and for two of every kind of animal. Noah looked at it with pride, his heart full of hope. He knew that soon, God's promise would come true. The animals would come, the rain would fall, and they would be ready.

Little did Noah know, this was just the beginning of a great adventure, one that would take them through storms and rainbows, through floods and new beginnings. It was a story of faith, of listening to the One True God, and of trusting in a promise as old as the world itself.

# 1

# A Special Message from the One True God

Noah wiped the sweat from his brow and looked out over the fields. It had been a long, hot day, and the sun was beginning to dip toward the horizon, painting the sky with shades of orange and pink. He sighed and leaned on his staff, feeling the weariness in his bones. But even in his tiredness, Noah felt a deep peace in his heart. He knew that God was watching over him, guiding his steps each day.

As the evening breeze rustled the leaves of the trees, Noah decided to sit down and rest. He found a spot under his favorite tree, an old oak that provided plenty of shade. The coolness of the grass beneath him was a welcome relief, and he closed his eyes, letting the sounds of nature fill his ears—the chirping of crickets, the gentle rustling of leaves, and the distant song of a bird.

It was In this peaceful moment that Noah heard a voice. It wasn't loud or harsh; it was gentle and kind, like a whisper that touched his heart. "Noah," the voice said, "I have something important to tell you."

Noah's eyes flew open, and he looked around, but he saw no one. Yet, he knew this voice. It was the voice of the One True God, the same voice that had guided him all his life. Noah took a deep breath, his heart beating fast. "I am here, Lord," he said, his voice steady. "What do You wish to tell me?"

The voice of God continued, and Noah listened carefully, his mind and heart open to every word. "The world has become full of violence and wickedness," God said. "People have turned away from Me and have chosen to live in ways that are harmful and unkind. I am saddened by what I see, and I have decided to cleanse the earth with a great flood.

But Noah, you have been faithful. You have walked with Me and lived a life that pleases Me. I want you to build an ark, a great boat, to save your family and two of every kind of animal. You will keep them safe, and when the waters recede, you will start a new life on a cleansed earth."

Noah's mind raced with the weight of what he was hearing. A great flood? An ark? Saving animals? It seemed like an impossible task, but Noah knew that when God spoke, it was important to listen and obey. He nodded, his heart filled with a mix of awe and determination. "I will do as You say, Lord," Noah replied. "I will build the ark, and I will follow Your instructions."

As the voice of God faded, Noah felt a deep sense of peace wash over him. He knew that he was not alone. God was with him, and together, they would do what needed to be done. Noah stood up, his heart filled with resolve. He had work to do, and he would do it with all his might.

Noah hurried home to tell his family the incredible news. As he entered his house, his wife looked up from her work, her eyes filled with curiosity. "Noah," she said, "you look like you've seen a vision. What's happened?"

Noah took a deep breath and began to tell his wife everything God had said. He spoke of the coming flood, the ark, and the plan to save the animals. His wife listened intently, her eyes widening with each word. When Noah finished, there was a moment of silence as she took it all in.

"An ark?" she finally said, her voice a mixture of surprise and concern. "Noah, do you know how big that would have to be? How will we do it?"

Noah smiled gently. "I don't have all the answers," he admitted, "but I trust in God's plan. He will show us the way. We will do this together, as a family, and God will be with us every step of the way."

His wife nodded, her trust in Noah and in God unwavering. "Then let's start," she said firmly. "There's no time to lose."

The next day, Noah gathered his sons—Shem, Ham, and Japheth—and told them about the great task that lay ahead. They listened with wide eyes, their expressions a mix of excitement and awe. "We'll help you, Father," Shem said, his voice filled with determination. "We'll build this ark, just as God has commanded."

With his family by his side, Noah set to work. They cut down trees, shaped the wood, and began to build the ark. The sound of hammers and saws filled the air as the great boat began to take shape. Day after day, they worked from sunrise to sunset, their hearts filled with a sense of purpose and faith.

People from the nearby villages came to watch, their faces full of curiosity and disbelief. "What are you doing, Noah?" they asked, laughing. "Why are you building such a big boat in the middle of nowhere? There's no water here!"

Noah simply smiled and kept working. "God has told me to build this ark," he replied. "A great flood is coming, and this ark will save us."

The people shook their heads and walked away, thinking Noah was foolish. But Noah knew better. He knew that God's words were true, and he trusted in the plan. Each day, as the ark grew taller and stronger, Noah felt his faith grow too. He was doing what God had asked, and he knew that God would take care of the rest.

As the days passed, Noah's heart filled with hope. The ark was nearly complete, and soon, they would be ready. The animals would come, the rain would fall, and God's promise would be fulfilled. It was a big task, but Noah knew that with God's help, they would do it. Together, they would face the storm, and together, they would find a new beginning.

2

# Building the Biggest Boat Ever

With the message from God still fresh in his mind, Noah woke up early the next morning, ready to begin the most important task of his life. The sun was just peeking over the horizon, casting a golden light over the fields. Noah took a deep breath of the fresh morning air, feeling the weight of his responsibility but also the strength that came from knowing God was with him.

"Today is the day we start building the ark," Noah announced to his family over breakfast. His voice was firm and filled with purpose. His wife, sons, and their wives listened intently, their faces a mixture of determination and anticipation.

"What will we need, Father?" asked Japheth, the youngest of Noah's sons, his eyes wide with curiosity.

"We'll need lots of wood," Noah replied. "Strong, sturdy wood to build a boat big enough for all of us and for the animals that God will send."

His sons nodded, ready to help. Shem, Ham, and Japheth were strong and hardworking, just like their father. They knew this task would not be easy, but they were ready. They gathered their axes and saws, their hands steady and sure.

Together, they walked to the nearby forest, where tall trees stood like giants against the sky. Noah pointed to the trees that would be perfect for the ark, their trunks thick and straight. "These will do," he said. "Let's get to work."

The sound of axes striking wood echoed through the forest as Noah and his sons began to cut down the trees. Each swing of the axe was filled with purpose, each cut a step closer to building the ark that would save them. As the trees fell, Noah thanked God for providing what they needed.

Once the trees were cut, they used their saws to shape the wood into long, strong planks. It was hard work, and their muscles ached, but they didn't stop. The sun climbed higher in the sky, and the heat made sweat drip from their brows, but still, they worked. They knew that each piece of wood brought them closer to completing the ark.

Noah's wife and daughters-in-law brought water to refresh them, their eyes filled with pride. They watched as the men worked, knowing that they, too, had a part to play in God's plan. They prepared food, kept the camp in order, and helped in any way they could.

Days turned into weeks, and weeks into months. Slowly, the ark began to take shape. It was massive, with a strong, sturdy frame that rose high into the sky. Its beams were thick, and its sides were tall, ready to withstand the waves that would come. Noah made sure every piece of wood was perfect, every joint secure.

As the ark grew, so did the curiosity of the people around them. Villagers came to watch, their faces filled with wonder and disbelief. "What is this, Noah?" they asked, pointing to the massive structure. "Why are you building such a huge boat?"

Noah wiped his brow and looked at them with kind eyes. "A great flood is coming," he explained. "God has told me to build this ark to save my family and the animals. You should prepare yourselves too."

But the people just laughed. "A flood? Here? There's no water for miles!" they said, shaking their heads. "You're wasting your time, Noah."

Noah simply smiled and went back to work. He knew that God's words were true, even if others couldn't see it. He hammered nails, tightened ropes, and made sure the ark was as strong as it could be. His family worked by his side, their hearts full of faith and their hands busy with the work God had given them.

One day, as Noah was inspecting the ark, he heard the first distant rumble of thunder. He looked up at the sky, which was beginning to darken with clouds. A chill ran down his spine, but it wasn't fear he felt—it was a deep, steady resolve. The time was coming, just as God had said.

"Hurry," Noah called to his sons. "We must finish. The storm will be here soon."

The urgency in his voice spurred everyone to move faster. They worked late into the night, the light of their lanterns flickering against the darkening sky. They hammered the last nails, secured the final beams, and made sure every inch of the ark was ready.

Noah stepped back and looked at the ark. It stood tall and strong, a mighty vessel ready to face the storm. His heart swelled with pride and gratitude. They had done it. They had built the ark, just as God had commanded.

His family nodded, their eyes filled with the same faith and determination. They knew that the hardest part was still to come, but they were not afraid. They had built the ark, and they had God's promise. Together, they would face the storm, and together, they would find a new beginning.

# 3

# Two by Two: The Animal Parade Begins

The sky was dark with clouds, but no rain had fallen yet. The air was thick with the promise of the storm to come. Inside the ark, Noah and his family were busy making final preparations. They had food stored, water barrels filled, and everything they needed to survive the great flood that was coming. The ark was ready, but there was one more thing left to do.

"Noah," God's voice spoke softly in his heart, "it is time to bring the animals to the ark. Two by two, they will come, every kind of creature that I have made. You will keep them safe until the waters have receded, and the earth is dry again."

Noah nodded, his heart filled with awe. He had trusted in God's plan from the beginning, but even he could hardly believe what was about to happen. Animals, from the largest elephant to the smallest mouse, would come to the ark to be saved. It was a sight that would be remembered forever.

Noah called his family together, and they stood at the great door of the ark, watching as the first animals appeared. It was a sight like no other. From the forest, fields, and mountains, creatures of every kind began to make their way toward the ark. They came two by two, each pair walking side by side as if they had been summoned by a silent call.

"There!" Shem pointed, his eyes wide with amazement. "Look at those elephants! They're coming this way!"

Sure enough, two massive elephants lumbered toward the ark, their trunks swinging and their large ears flapping. Behind them came two graceful giraffes, their long necks stretching toward the sky. Noah's heart swelled with joy. It was happening just as God had said.

Noah's wife and daughters-in-law hurried to prepare the stalls for the animals. The ark was built with many rooms, each designed to hold different kinds of creatures. There were stalls for the large animals, pens for the smaller ones, and perches for the birds. Noah's sons helped guide the animals to their places, making sure each one was comfortable and safe.

As the day passed, more and more animals arrived. Lions and tigers padded softly on their big paws, their eyes shining in the dim light. Bears lumbered up the ramp, their thick fur shining in the light. Deer and antelope pranced lightly, their movements graceful and quick.

From the trees came monkeys, chattering and swinging from branch to branch. Birds flew overhead, their wings flapping as they landed gently on the ark. Peacocks, parrots, and sparrows—all the birds of the air—came to find shelter. Noah marveled at the variety and beauty of God's creatures.

And it wasn't just the big animals. Small creatures came too. Rabbits hopped through the grass, and squirrels scampered up the ark's ramp. Mice scurried along the ground, and insects buzzed in the air. Each one found its place, guided by an unseen hand.

Noah's family worked tirelessly, making sure every animal had food and water. They tended to the needs of the creatures, their hands gentle and caring. The ark was filled with the sounds of life—the roar of lions, the trumpeting of elephants, the chirping of birds. It was a symphony of nature, a reminder of the wonder and creativity of God's creation.

As the last of the animals made their way into the ark, Noah took a moment to look around. The great boat was alive with activity, every corner filled with the creatures they had worked so hard to save. It was a sight that filled him with awe and gratitude.

Noah looked up at the sky, the clouds thickening but no rain yet falling. He knew that the time was coming. It wouldn't be long now before the rain would start, just as God had said.

"It's time to enter the ark," Noah said to his family. They nodded, understanding the importance of the moment. They gathered together, stepping into the ark as a family. As they entered, the ark's massive door remained open, a symbol of their trust in God's plan.

Once everyone was inside, something extraordinary happened. Noah felt a sudden presence, a deep sense of peace that filled the ark. It was then that the door of the ark began to move, not by human hands, but by an invisible force. Slowly, with a deep, echoing sound, the door swung shut, sealing them safely inside.

Noah and his family watched in awe as the door closed. They knew without a doubt that it was God who had shut the door, protecting them from the flood that was to come. Inside the ark, the light was dim, lit by the soft glow of lanterns. The air was filled with the scent of hay and animals, a comforting smell that spoke of safety and warmth.

The days passed, and Noah and his family waited. The animals were calm, as if they too knew that God was with them. They spent their days tending to the creatures, making sure everyone was fed and cared for. The sky outside remained cloudy, a constant reminder of the coming storm.

Then, on the seventh day, Noah felt a change in the air. The sky grew darker, the wind began to howl, and the first drops of rain fell. It started as a gentle drizzle, but soon it became a steady downpour, a curtain of water that blurred the world outside. The sound of the rain filled the ark, a steady drumbeat against the wooden walls.

Inside, Noah and his family gathered together, their hearts filled with faith and trust. They had done as God had asked, and now they would wait, knowing that they were safe in His hands. The rain would fall for forty days and forty nights, but they were ready. With God's promise in their hearts, they would face the storm, knowing that a new beginning awaited them.

# 4

# Rain, Rain, Go Away

As the last of the animals settled into their places inside the ark, Noah stood at the great door, peering out at the darkening sky. The air was heavy with anticipation, and a hush had fallen over the land. It was as if the whole world was holding its breath, waiting for something to happen.

Noah's heart was filled with a mix of excitement and solemnity. He knew that the time had come. God's promise was about to unfold, and they were about to embark on a journey like no other. The ark was ready, the animals were safe, and now, all they could do was wait.

The first raindrop fell, a single bead of water that landed on Noah's hand. He looked up, watching as more drops began to fall, dotting the ground and creating tiny ripples in the puddles that quickly formed. The rain came gently at first, a soft patter that barely made a sound. But soon, it grew steadier, the drops larger, and the patter turning into a steady drumbeat against the wooden roof of the ark.

Noah turned to his family, who were gathered inside, their eyes wide with awe. "It has begun," he said softly. "The rain is here."

His wife and sons nodded, their faces a mixture of wonder and seriousness. They knew the significance of this moment. It was the start of the great flood, the beginning of the journey that God had prepared them for. They watched as the rain fell, faster and heavier, turning the ground into a sea of mud.

Inside the ark, the animals stirred, sensing the change in the air. The lions growled softly, the elephants trumpeted, and the birds chirped nervously. Noah and his family moved through the ark, calming the animals, making sure each one was comfortable and secure. They spoke in soothing tones, their hands gentle as they reassured the creatures that they were safe.

The rain continued to fall, a steady, unending cascade of water. The ark rocked gently as the ground beneath it softened and the waters rose. Noah could feel the ark lift, the sensation of floating as it was carried by the rising floodwaters. He knew that they were in God's hands, guided by His plan.

Days passed, and still, the rain fell. It poured from the heavens, turning the world outside into a vast ocean. The ark floated on the water, rocked by the waves but held steady by God's protection. Inside, Noah and his family kept busy, caring for the animals, tending to their needs, and making sure everything was in order.

Noah stood by one of the small windows of the ark, looking out at the endless sea. The world as he had known it was gone, covered by the waters of the flood. But Noah was not afraid. He knew that God was with them, guiding them through the storm. He felt a deep sense of peace, knowing that they were exactly where they were meant to be.

At night, as the rain drummed against the roof, Noah and his family would gather together, their hearts filled with faith. They prayed, thanking God for His protection, for the ark that kept them safe, and for the promise of a new beginning. They knew that the rain would not last forever, that one day, the waters would recede, and they would step out into a new world.

The sound of the rain became a familiar rhythm, a lullaby that lulled them to sleep each night. It was a reminder of God's power, of the great cleansing that was taking place. Noah knew that the rain was part of God's plan, a necessary step in the journey that would lead to a brighter future.

As the days turned into weeks, the rain continued, a constant presence that filled the air. The ark floated on, carried by the waters, guided by God's hand. Inside, there was peace, there was love, and there was the promise of a new beginning.

Noah's heart was filled with gratitude as he looked at his family, at the animals that filled the ark, and at the rain that fell outside. He knew that they were part of a story that would be told for generations to come, a story of faith, of trust, and of a love that would never fade.

And so, they waited, trusting in God's timing, knowing that the rain would one day stop, that the storm would pass, and that the sun would shine again. They knew that they were safe, that they were loved, and that they were exactly where they were meant to be.

The rain fell, the ark floated, and the adventure continued, a journey that would take them through the storm and into a new world. It was a journey that was just beginning, a journey that would change everything.

# 5

# 40 Days and 40 Nights: A Floating World

The rain poured down in heavy sheets, drumming against the roof of the ark and turning the world outside into a gray, swirling sea. The sky was dark, the clouds thick and heavy, and the wind howled through the trees. It was a storm like no other, and the sound of the rain was so loud that it seemed to fill every corner of the ark.

Inside the ark, Noah and his family could feel the great boat rocking gently on the rising waters. At first, it was just a slow, gentle sway, but as the rain continued to fall, the ark began to lift, floating higher and higher. Noah stood by one of the small windows, looking out into the storm. He could see the water rising, covering the land and the trees. The world outside was disappearing, swallowed up by the flood.

"God is with us," Noah said, his voice calm and steady. "He has promised to keep us safe, and we must trust in His plan."

His wife and sons nodded, their faces showing their faith and determination. They had worked hard to build the ark, and now they were seeing the reason for all their labor. The rain was falling, just as God had said, but they were safe inside the ark, surrounded by the creatures they had saved.

As the days passed, the rain continued to fall. The ark rose higher and higher, floating on the endless sea. Inside, the animals were calm, sensing that they were protected. Noah and his family took turns caring for the animals, making sure they had enough food and water. The lions roared softly in their cages, the elephants trumpeted gently, and the birds sang sweetly from their perches. It was a strange and wonderful sight, a floating zoo in the middle of the storm.

Noah's sons worked hard to keep everything in order. Shem, Ham, and Japheth moved through the ark, checking on the animals and making sure everything was secure. They carried hay to the stalls, filled water troughs, and cleaned up the messes that the animals made. It was hard work, but they did it with a sense of purpose, knowing that they were part of God's plan.

One evening, as the rain continued to pour, Noah gathered his family together. They sat in a circle, the warm light of the lanterns casting soft shadows on the walls of the ark. The sound of the rain was a constant background noise, but inside, it was peaceful and calm.

"We must remember why we are here," Noah said, his voice steady and strong. "God has chosen us to save His creation, to start a new beginning. We must trust in Him, even when the storm is all around us."

His family nodded, their faces showing their trust and faith. They knew that they were part of something greater, a story that would be told for generations to come. They held hands and prayed together, asking God for strength and guidance.

The days turned Into weeks, and still, the rain fell. The ark floated on the endless sea, with no land in sight. The water covered everything, a vast, endless expanse that stretched as far as the eye could see. But inside the ark, there was life, a small, floating world filled with the sounds of animals and the prayers of a faithful family.

One day, as Noah was looking out the window, he noticed something strange. The rain was beginning to slow. The steady downpour was turning into a light drizzle, and the dark clouds were starting to break apart. A faint light shone through the clouds, a small glimpse of the sun that had been hidden for so long.

"Look!" Noah called to his family, his voice filled with excitement. "The rain is stopping!"

They all rushed to the windows, their eyes wide with wonder. The rain was indeed slowing, the drops falling less heavily now, and the sky was beginning to clear. The endless storm was finally coming to an end.

Noah's heart swelled with hope. They had been in the ark for forty days and forty nights, floating on the floodwaters. But now, the rain was stopping, and a new chapter was beginning. He knew that they still had a journey ahead of them, but this was a sign, a promise that the worst was over.

As the rain stopped and the clouds began to part, a sense of peace filled the ark. The sun broke through, casting a warm, golden light over the water. The ark floated gently, rocked by the waves, but it was steady and strong.

Noah gathered his family, and they stood together, looking out at the clearing sky. They knew that they were not alone. God was with them, guiding them through the storm, and now, leading them to a new beginning.

They would wait patiently, trusting in God's timing. The waters would recede, and the earth would dry. They would send out a dove to find dry land, and when the time was right, they would step out of the ark Into a world washed clean, ready to start anew.

For now, they would rest, knowing that they were safe in God's hands. The storm had passed, and a new day was dawning. It was a day filled with hope, a day that marked the beginning of a new life, a new world, and a promise that would never be forgotten.

# 6

# The Search for Dry Land

The rain had finally stopped, and the clouds were beginning to part, revealing a bright blue sky. The sun shone down, warming the ark's wooden deck and casting golden light through the small windows. After forty days and forty nights of rain, the storm had passed. The world was silent, except for the gentle creaking of the ark as it floated on the endless waters.

Inside the ark, Noah and his family were filled with hope. They had waited patiently, trusting in God's promise, and now they felt that the time was near. The ark was still surrounded by water, but they knew that somewhere out there, the earth was beginning to dry. It was time to see if the land was ready.

"We should send out a bird," Noah said one morning, his eyes bright with anticipation. "If the bird finds dry land, it will bring back a sign."

His family nodded, understanding the importance of the task. Noah chose a dove, a gentle, white bird with bright eyes. He held the dove carefully in his hands, feeling its soft feathers against his skin. The dove cooed softly, as if it understood the important mission it was about to undertake.

"Go, find us a sign," Noah whispered to the dove, his voice filled with hope. He walked to one of the small windows of the ark, opened it, and gently released the dove into the air.

The dove spread its wings and soared into the sky, circling the ark before flying off into the distance. Noah watched it go, his heart filled with a mix of excitement and nerves. Would the dove find dry land? Would it bring back a sign that the earth was ready for them to return?

The family waited, their eyes fixed on the sky, hoping to see the dove's return. Hours passed, and the sun began to set, casting a warm glow over the water. Finally, as the last light of day faded, they saw a small shape against the sky. The dove was returning!

Noah's heart leaped with joy as the dove flew back to the ark. It landed on his outstretched arm, its feathers ruffled but its eyes bright. But the dove's feet were empty—it had found no place to rest. The waters still covered the earth.

Noah's heart sank a little, but he didn't lose hope. He knew that God's timing was perfect, and they just needed to wait a little longer. "Thank you, brave dove," Noah said softly, stroking its feathers. "We will try again."

Seven days later, Noah decided to send the dove out again. This time, as he released the bird into the air, his heart was filled with a quiet confidence. He knew that they were closer to the day when they would leave the ark and begin their new life.

The family watched the dove fly away, its white wings shining against the blue sky. They prayed together, asking God to guide the dove and bring back a sign. They knew that God had a plan, and they trusted Him completely.

As the day went on, they continued their work, caring for the animals and keeping the ark in order. The sun was warm, and the air was filled with the sounds of birds chirping, lions roaring, and elephants trumpeting. It was a reminder of the life that God had saved, the life that would soon fill the earth again.

As the sun began to set, they saw a small white shape in the sky. The dove was returning! This time, Noah could see something in its beak, a small, green branch. His heart raced with excitement as the dove landed gently on his arm.

An olive branch! The dove had brought back a sign of life, a sign that the waters were receding and that dry land was near. Noah's eyes filled with tears of joy as he held the dove and the olive branch.

"Look!" he called to his family, his voice filled with happiness. "The dove has brought back an olive branch! God has kept His promise! The earth is drying, and soon we will be able to leave the ark."

His family gathered around, their faces shining with joy. They knew that this was a sign from God, a promise that the worst was over. They hugged each other, their hearts filled with gratitude and hope.

For the next seven days, Noah and his family watched the sky, knowing that their time in the ark was coming to an end. They thanked God for His protection and for guiding them through the storm. They prepared for the day when they would step out of the ark and onto dry land, ready to start a new chapter in their lives.

Finally, Noah decided to send the dove out one last time. As he released it into the air, he knew that this would be the final test. The dove flew into the sky, its wings beating strongly, and disappeared over the horizon.

They waited, watching the sky, their hearts filled with anticipation. But this time, the dove did not return. Noah smiled, understanding the message. The dove had found a place to rest, a place where it could make a home. The earth was ready.

Noah turned to his family, his face glowing with joy. "God has given us a sign," he said, his voice filled with emotion. "The dove has found dry land. Soon, we will leave the ark and begin our new life."

His family cheered, their hearts overflowing with happiness. They knew that God had guided them through the storm, and now, He was leading them to a new beginning. They had trusted in His promise, and now, that promise was being fulfilled.

As the sun set, casting a golden light over the water, Noah and his family stood together, looking out at the world that awaited them. They knew that their journey was not yet over, but they were ready. With God's guidance, they would step out of the ark, onto dry land, and start a new life filled with hope, faith, and love.

7

# A Grateful Offering: Honoring God's Blessings

As the ark came to rest on the mountains of Ararat and the floodwaters began to recede, Noah and his family felt a deep sense of gratitude. They had been through so much—the building of the ark, the gathering of the animals, and the long days and nights of rain. Now, after all those months, they were finally stepping out onto solid ground, a world washed clean by the great flood.

The air was fresh, filled with the scent of damp earth and new growth. The sun shone brightly, casting its warm light over the land, and a gentle breeze rustled the leaves of the trees. Everywhere Noah looked, he saw signs of new life. Plants were sprouting, birds were singing, and the animals, finally free from the ark, roamed the land.

Noah's heart was full of thankfulness. He knew that it was God's mercy and love that had saved them. It was God's plan that had guided them through the storm, and now, it was God's promise of a new beginning that lay before them. Noah wanted to show his gratitude in a special way, to honor God for His protection and care.

As his family gathered around, Noah felt a deep need to thank God. He decided to build an altar, a place where he could offer a sacrifice to the One True God. It would be a way to say thank you, a way to show God how much

23

they appreciated His love and mercy.

Noah," said Shem, as they worked together to gather stones, "why are we building this altar?"

"We are building this altar to give thanks to God," Noah replied, his voice filled with reverence. "God has kept us safe through the flood. He has given us a new beginning, a chance to start over. We must honor Him and show our gratitude."

The family worked together, piling stones into a sturdy altar. They gathered wood and prepared everything carefully. Noah chose the best of the clean animals for the sacrifice, a sign of his respect and love for God. When everything was ready, Noah stood before the altar, his heart full of devotion.

With solemn hands, Noah laid the animal on the altar and lit the fire. The flames rose high, and the smoke curled up into the sky, a pleasing aroma that filled the air. As the sacrifice burned, Noah bowed his head, his heart overflowing with thankfulness.

"Lord God, Creator of heaven and earth," Noah prayed, his voice strong and clear, "we thank You for Your love and mercy. You have saved us from the flood, guided us through the storm, and given us a new beginning. We offer this sacrifice as a sign of our gratitude. May our hearts always be filled with love for You, and may we always live in a way that pleases You."

As Noah prayed, the smoke from the sacrifice rose higher, blending with the clouds. It was a sign of his devotion, a sign that he honored God with all his heart. Noah knew that God was pleased with their offering, that God heard their prayers and was with them.

After the sacrifice, Noah and his family stood together, looking up at the sky. They knew that God had seen their offering, that He was pleased with their devotion. They felt a deep sense of peace, knowing that they were loved and protected by the One True God.

As they stood there, something beautiful happened. The sky, which had been clear and blue, was now painted with a brilliant rainbow. It stretched across the sky, a perfect arch of colors, brighter and more beautiful than they had ever seen.

Noah's eyes filled with tears as he looked at the rainbow. It was a sign of

God's promise, a promise that He would never again send a flood to cover the earth. It was a sign of God's love, a love that would never fade, a love that would always be there.

"Look," Noah said, his voice filled with wonder. "God has given us a sign. The rainbow is His promise, a promise that He will always be with us, guiding us and protecting us. It is a sign of His love, a love that will never end."

His family looked up at the rainbow, their hearts filled with joy. They knew that they were not alone, that God was with them, watching over them and guiding their steps. The rainbow was a reminder of God's faithfulness, a promise that would never be broken.

With hearts filled with gratitude, Noah and his family walked back to their home, the rainbow shining brightly above them. They knew that they had been given a great gift, a gift of love and hope. They knew that they were part of something special, a story that would be told for generations to come.

They would honor God's promise, and they would live their lives with faith and kindness. They would remember the rainbow, the symbol of God's love, a love that would never end. And they would teach their children and their children's children to remember God's promises, to live their lives with love and faith, just as Noah had taught them.

# 8

# Conclusion

As Noah and his family settled into their new lives, they never forgot the incredible journey they had taken. The ark, the flood, the animals, and the rainbow—all these memories were forever etched in their hearts. They knew they were part of a story that was much bigger than themselves, a story of faith, courage, and trust in the One True God.

Every time a rainbow appeared in the sky, Noah and his family would stop and look up, their hearts filled with joy and gratitude. It was a reminder of God's promise, a promise that He would never again flood the earth. The rainbow was a beautiful sign of God's love, stretching across the sky in brilliant colors, a promise that could be seen by all.

Noah's grandchildren loved to hear the story of the ark. They would sit at his feet, eyes wide with wonder, as he told them about the great boat, the animals coming two by two, and the forty days and nights of rain. They could almost hear the sound of the animals, the roar of the lions, the trumpeting of the elephants, and the sweet songs of the birds. They imagined the ark floating on the endless sea, rocking gently on the waves, safe and secure in God's care.

As they grew older, Noah's children and grandchildren remembered his words. They lived their lives with love and kindness, trusting in God's plan. They taught their own children about the ark and the rainbow, about the promise that God had made. They passed down the story from generation to generation, a story that was filled with hope and faith.

Noah knew that the story of the ark was more than just a tale of survival. It was a story of God's love for His creation, a love that was as wide as the sky and as deep as the ocean. It was a story that showed the importance of listening to God, of obeying His voice, and of trusting in His promises. Noah's faith had been tested, but he had remained strong, and God had rewarded him with a new beginning.

The land around them flourished, filled with green fields, tall trees, and animals of every kind. The air was filled with the sound of life, a symphony of God's creation. Noah's family thrived, growing and spreading out, filling the earth with love and kindness. They knew that they were part of something special, a story that would be told for generations to come.

Noah's life was long, and he saw his children's children grow up, each one a part of the promise that God had made. As he watched them play, their laughter filling the air, he knew that the story of the ark would live on. It was a story of faith, of trust, and of a love that would never end.

And so, every time the rain fell and a rainbow appeared in the sky, Noah's family would remember. They would remember the ark, the flood, and the promise of the One True God. They would look up at the rainbow, a sign of God's everlasting love, and they would smile, knowing that they were part of a story that would never fade, a story that would live on forever.

# Epilogue

**The Legacy of Noah's Faith**

Years passed, and Noah's hair turned silver, his hands weathered with the work of a long, faithful life. His heart, however, remained as strong and steady as the ark he had built so many years ago. Surrounded by his children, grandchildren, and even great-grandchildren, Noah felt a deep sense of peace. He knew that his family would continue to live with the same faith and trust in God that had guided him.

The land around them had flourished. The fields were golden with wheat, the orchards heavy with fruit, and the rivers ran clear and full. Animals roamed freely, from the gentle deer to the mighty lions, each one a testament to the new life that had begun after the flood. Noah's descendants had spread out, building homes and communities, each one a light of God's love in the world.

Noah would often sit with his family, sharing stories of the days before the flood, the great ark, and the promise of the rainbow. The children never tired of hearing how God had spoken to Noah, guiding him to build the ark, and how the animals had come two by two. They would listen in awe as Noah described the forty days and nights of rain, the endless sea, and the joy of seeing the first sign of land.

One evening, as the sun was setting and the sky was painted with hues of pink and gold, Noah gathered his family around him. He looked at their faces, filled with love and hope, and knew that his journey was almost at its end. But he was not afraid. He had lived a good life, a life filled with faith and obedience to the One True God.

"My dear family," Noah said, his voice soft but clear, "always remember the story of the ark. Remember how God guided us, protected us, and gave us a new beginning. Remember the promise of the rainbow, a sign of God's love that will never fade. Live your lives with kindness and love, and trust in God's plan. Teach your children to listen to God's voice, to obey His commands, and to have faith, even when the way is not clear."

His family nodded, their eyes filled with tears. They knew that Noah's words were true, that his life had been a shining example of faith. They promised to honor his legacy, to live as he had lived, trusting in God's love and following His guidance.

As the stars appeared in the night sky, a gentle breeze rustled the leaves of the trees. Noah looked up, a smile on his face. He knew that he had done what God had asked, that he had fulfilled his purpose. He knew that his family would carry on the story, that they would continue to live in faith and love.

The world was a different place now, a place filled with hope and promise. The legacy of Noah's faith lived on, in the hearts of his children, and in the hearts of all who would come after. The rainbow, a symbol of God's promise, stretched across the sky, a reminder of a love that would never end.

Noah closed his eyes, his heart filled with peace. He knew that the story of the ark, the flood, and the promise would be told for generations to come. It was a story of faith, a story of trust, and a story of a love that would never fade. It was a story that would live on, a legacy of faith that would shine like the stars in the sky, a beacon of hope for all who would follow.

# Afterword

**A Message for Young Hearts**

**Dear Readers,**

Thank you for joining us on this incredible journey through Noah's Big Boat Adventure: Saving the Animals. Noah's story is one of faith, courage, and trust in the One True God. It teaches us that even in the midst of storms, when the world seems uncertain and dark, we can trust that God is with us, guiding us, and protecting us.

Noah's world was a difficult place, filled with people who had forgotten to be kind and good. But Noah chose to listen to God's voice. He chose to live with love, to obey God's commands, and to trust in God's plan. Because of Noah's faith, God gave him a special mission—to save his family and the animals, to build a new world filled with hope and promise.

Imagine building a boat so big it could hold every kind of animal, floating on an endless sea, and waiting for the rain to stop. Imagine the joy of seeing the first sign of dry land, the beauty of stepping out into a new world, and the awe of seeing a rainbow stretched across the sky. Noah's story shows us that when we trust in God, even the most impossible tasks become possible.

The rainbow is a symbol of God's promise, a promise that He will always be with us, that He will never again send a flood to cover the earth. It is a reminder of God's love, a love that is as wide as the sky and as deep as the ocean. Whenever you see a rainbow, remember that God's love is with you, guiding you, and protecting you.

Noah's story is not just a story from long ago. It is a story that lives on in each of us. It is a story that reminds us to live with kindness, to trust in God's plan, and to have faith, even when the way is not clear. It is a story that shows us the importance of listening to God's voice and following His guidance.

As you go through life, remember the lessons of Noah's story. Be kind, be loving, and be faithful. Trust in God's promises, and know that He is always with you. Teach others about God's love, and pass down the story of the ark, the flood, and the rainbow to future generations. Let your life be a beacon of hope, a light that shines brightly, just like the rainbow in the sky.

Thank you for being part of this journey. May Noah's story fill your heart with hope and faith, and may you always remember that you are part of a story that is filled with love, a story that will never end.

With love and blessings,

Michael Southern Sr